World 🌐 Cities

NEW YORK

Christine Hatt

*Special photography
by Chris Fairclough*

This edition published in 2002 by

Belitha Press

a member of Chrysalis Books Plc.
64 Brewery Road, London N7 9NT

ISBN 1 84138 736 3 (hb)
ISBN 1 84138 737 1 (pb)

British Library Cataloguing in Publication Data
for this book is available from the British Library.

Printed in Hong Kong

Editor Stephanie Turnbull
Designer Helen James
Photographer Chris Fairclough
Map illustrator Lorraine Harrison
Picture researcher Kathy Lockley
Consultant Dr Matthew Gandy, University College London

Additional images
Art Directors & TRIP Photo Library/Malcolm Lee: 14b;
Richard Berenholtz/CORBIS: 4cl; Gail Mooney/CORBIS 37t;
Bettmann/CORBIS 41tl; Robert Harding Picture Library: 13t,
13b, 18t, 26b, 39b, 42b; Nan Melville: 34b; Peter Newark's
American Pictures: 8t, 9b, 9t, 10b, 11t, 26t, 27t, 35t, 40b; North
Wind Picture Archives: 8b, 10t, 24t, 40t; Rex Features: Steve
Wood 11b; 36t, 38t, 38t, 38b, 41cr, 41bl, David Rentas 43cl; 43b;
Frank Spooner Pictures: 11b, 12t, 17b, 27b, 39t, 42t; Sporting
Pictures: 35b.

Words in **bold** are explained in the glossary on pages 46 and 47.

CONTENTS

INTRODUCTION

New York City is on the east coast of the USA, in the south-eastern corner of New York State. It has a population of over seven million, the largest of any city in the country, and an area of 783 square kilometres. Four of its boroughs (Manhattan, Staten Island, Brooklyn and Queens) are completely or partly on islands in Hudson River, East River and New York Bay. Most of the fifth borough, the Bronx, is on the mainland.

The Big Apple

'The Big Apple' was a term probably first used by jazz musicians to mean any large city. Now the nickname refers only to New York, with its unique style and energy. New Yorkers often claim that their city's lively streets, busy shops, excellent cultural life and dynamic financial district make it the most exciting place on Earth. The New York skyline, with its sleek skyscrapers, is a worldwide symbol of big city life.

▲ Many gleaming skyscrapers, full of offices and apartments, tower over New York. This unique skyline is instantly recognizable to other people all over the world.

Grid system

People can find their way around easily in New York because most of the city's roads are built on a grid system (see page 10). Numbered streets run from right to left and numbered avenues go up and down. There are some exceptions to this rule, for example the famous road called Broadway, which runs diagonally across much of Manhattan.

NEW YORK

STATUS
Most highly populated city in the USA;
headquarters of the United Nations

AREA
783 square kilometres

POPULATION
7.42 million (1998)

GOVERNMENT
Elected mayor, borough presidents and council

CLIMATE
Average temperatures range from
-3°C in January to 29°C in July

TIME ZONE
Eastern Standard Time
(**Greenwich Mean Time** minus 5 hours)

CURRENCY
US Dollar ($); 1 dollar = 100 cents

OFFICIAL LANGUAGE
English

A multicultural city

New York has always been home to people of many nationalities. Now old-established Irish, Italian, Jewish and African-American communities mingle with groups who have arrived more recently from places such as Honduras and El Salvador. In areas such as Chinatown (see page 13), members of the same race live together. Elsewhere, languages and lifestyles mix to make New York a truly multicultural city.

➤ The Statue of Liberty is the most famous symbol of New York. It was made in France then shipped to New York and unveiled in 1886.

◄ City Hall, in south-eastern Manhattan. This is where the mayor works and where public events and celebrations are sometimes held.

City government

New York City is governed by an elected mayor (see page 41), whose offices are in City Hall and whose official residence is Gracie Mansion. The mayor is assisted by five borough presidents, a 51-member council and a huge staff. New York also houses the headquarters of the **United Nations**, which overlook East River. This allows the city to declare proudly that it is the 'capital of the world'.

MAPS OF THE CITY

These maps show New York as it is today. The area map shows all five New York boroughs and the surrounding region. The street map gives a close-up view of Manhattan borough, the heart of New York City. Many of the places mentioned in the book are marked.

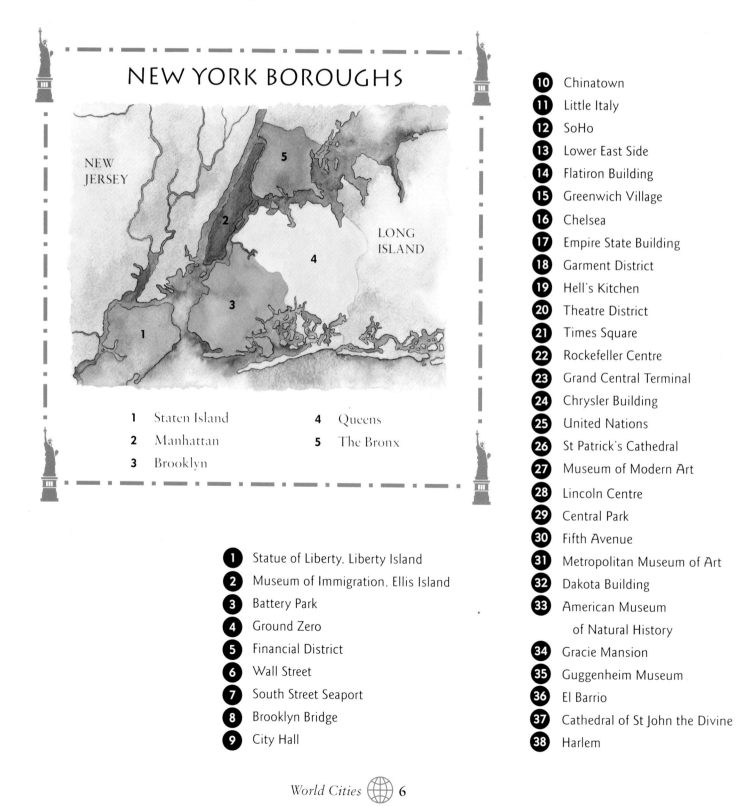

NEW YORK BOROUGHS

NEW JERSEY

LONG ISLAND

1	Staten Island	4	Queens
2	Manhattan	5	The Bronx
3	Brooklyn		

1 Statue of Liberty, Liberty Island
2 Museum of Immigration, Ellis Island
3 Battery Park
4 Ground Zero
5 Financial District
6 Wall Street
7 South Street Seaport
8 Brooklyn Bridge
9 City Hall

10 Chinatown
11 Little Italy
12 SoHo
13 Lower East Side
14 Flatiron Building
15 Greenwich Village
16 Chelsea
17 Empire State Building
18 Garment District
19 Hell's Kitchen
20 Theatre District
21 Times Square
22 Rockefeller Centre
23 Grand Central Terminal
24 Chrysler Building
25 United Nations
26 St Patrick's Cathedral
27 Museum of Modern Art
28 Lincoln Centre
29 Central Park
30 Fifth Avenue
31 Metropolitan Museum of Art
32 Dakota Building
33 American Museum
   of Natural History
34 Gracie Mansion
35 Guggenheim Museum
36 El Barrio
37 Cathedral of St John the Divine
38 Harlem

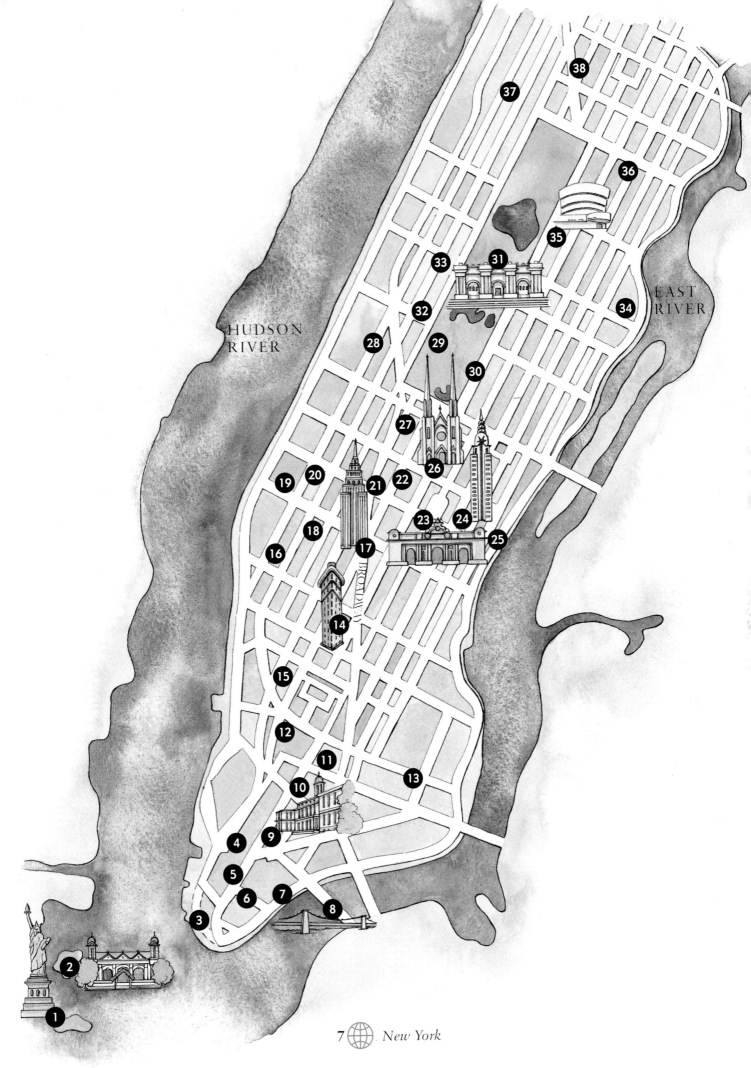

HUDSON
RIVER

EAST
RIVER

BROADWAY

NEW YORK'S EARLY HISTORY

The first inhabitants of the area where New York now lies were Native Americans. They belonged to tribes of the **Algonquian** family and later also of the **Iroquois** family. Their traditional ways of life changed after Europeans settled in the region in the 17th century.

Early exploration

In 1524 the Italian explorer Giovanni da Verrazzano sailed along America's east coast and became the first European to see the future site of New York. In 1609 Englishman Henry Hudson landed on Manhattan Island, then sailed 240 kilometres down the river later named after him. Hudson worked for a trading organization called the Dutch West India Company. In 1624 the company set up the Dutch **colony** of New Netherlands in the area that Hudson had explored.

▲ This village, made up of wooden **longhouses**, belonged to the Algonquian Wappinger tribe. They lived on Manhattan Island before the arrival of the Dutch in the 17th century.

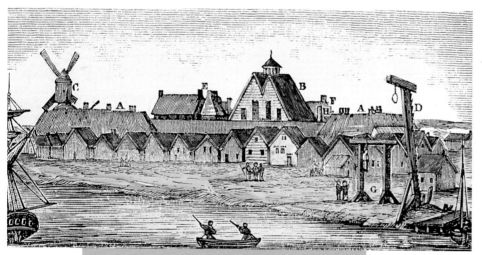

▲ The Dutch city of New Amsterdam in 1659. Its buildings included a church (centre) and a windmill (far left).

New Amsterdam

Many Dutch families settled in the New Netherlands area. In 1625 some moved to the southern end of Manhattan Island and founded a town called New Amsterdam. A year later, Dutchman Peter Minuit became governor of the town. Minuit then bought Manhattan from the Native Americans for cloth and beads.

Peter Stuyvesant

During the 17th century, people settled in areas around Manhattan that later became the four other boroughs of New York City (see page 6). At the same time, New Amsterdam spread north. In 1646 Peter Stuyvesant became the stern new governor of the town. He made it a city in 1653 and built a wooden defensive wall along its northern edge. Wall Street, in New York's Financial District (see page 25), now marks the place where the wall stood.

New York

The British had colonies in North America and wanted New Amsterdam too, so in 1664 they sent four warships to seize the city. They succeeded easily as the Dutch West India Company did not defend the colony. The inhabitants of New Amsterdam did not oppose the British either, as they hated the strict laws that Peter Stuyvesant had passed. The British renamed the city New York after James, Duke of York, the brother of British king Charles II.

▲ Peter Stuyvesant improved the New Amsterdam settlement in many ways. For example, he built its first hospital and paved its roads.

▲ In 1783, when the defeated British troops had left New York, George Washington entered the city in triumph.

The American Revolution

Many New Yorkers and other Americans did not want to be ruled by a British government far away in London. In 1775 they began a revolution, led by **George Washington**, to end British rule. In 1776 the British won several battles in New York. They took over the city, but were defeated elsewhere and in 1783 gave up their North American colonies. In 1789 New York became the capital of the newly formed USA and Washington was sworn in there as the country's first president.

AFTER THE REVOLUTION

In 1790 Philadelphia took over as the American capital. But New York still grew amazingly fast – in ten years the population rose by 30,000 to reach 79,000 in 1800. This growth continued throughout the 19th century and beyond.

Growth and change

In 1811 a new plan for the city was devised that divided the land above 14th Street into a grid. This still forms the basis of the city's layout. Another important event was the opening of the Erie Canal in 1825. Goods for shipping overseas were brought along the canal to New York, which grew into a major seaport. In 1842 the Croton **Aqueduct** brought pure water to the city for the first time. Then in 1858 Central Park was laid out (see page 16). This was the largest park in the country.

▲ The 585-kilometre-long, 12-metre-wide Erie Canal was built in just seven years. It linked New York's Hudson River to the **Great Lakes**.

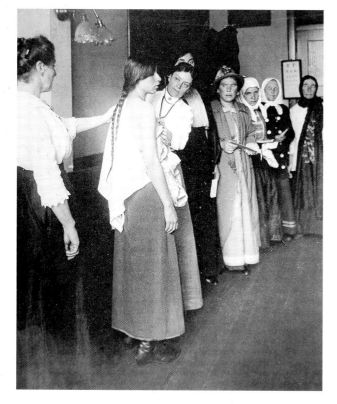

New arrivals

From the 1820s, thousands of European **immigrants** poured into New York City. The pace of immigration grew faster in mid-century, after famine in Ireland (see page 12) and revolution in Germany led people to seek refuge abroad. Immigrant numbers increased further still from the 1880s, when Jews escaping ill-treatment in Eastern Europe and Russia arrived in the city. Poor Italians also came to New York looking for work.

◄ Immigrants at Ellis Island in 1900 (see page 37). People arriving there had to have a medical examination. If they were suffering from an infectious disease, they were sent back home.

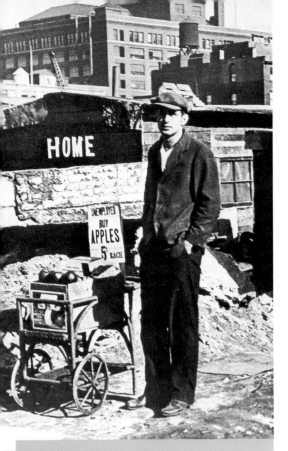

▲ About 25 per cent of New Yorkers were unemployed in the 1930s' depression. They sold their belongings to make money, but many people lost their homes and had to live in **shantytowns**.

The Civil War and after

From 1861 to 1865 the North of the USA, including New York, took part in a **civil war** against the South. There was not much fighting in the city, although terrible **race riots** broke out in 1863, mainly between Irish and black Americans. The North won the war and New York thrived again, but its government was controlled by the corrupt **Tammany Society**. The society became less powerful after its leader, William Marcy Tweed (see page 26), was imprisoned in 1873.

The 20th century

In the late 19th century New York covered little more than Manhattan Island. Then in 1898 it joined Queens, Brooklyn, Staten Island and the Bronx to form Greater New York, the modern city. As the 20th century began, skyscrapers sprang up and the city boomed. The boom ended in 1929 when the **Wall Street Crash** (see page 25) brought economic **depression**. New York slowly recovered and after the **Second World War** more immigrants flooded in, many from Puerto Rico (see page 13).

September 11

New York has faced many problems since the 1950s. In 1964 there were race riots in Harlem, and in 1975 the city went bankrupt. But on 11 September, 2001, New York endured its worst tragedy yet. In the morning of that day, Arab terrorists flew two passenger aeroplanes into the World Trade Centre (see page 15). By 10.30 a.m. both of its towers had collapsed, and about 2800 people, including more than 300 firefighters, were dead. Despite their grief, New Yorkers are determined that their city will recover.

Two firefighters ➤ stumble through the wreckage of the World Trade Centre. Hundreds of them rushed to the scene when the south tower fell. Many were then killed when the north tower collapsed.

THE PEOPLE OF NEW YORK

The population of New York has contained members of many races ever since the 17th century. Now about 40 per cent of its inhabitants are **immigrants** or have parents who were.

The Irish population

Thousands of Irish people came to New York in the mid-19th century when famine hit Ireland. Many settled in an area of Manhattan called Hell's Kitchen, where they lived in poverty. Now the city's Irish population is huge – more Irish people live in New York than in Dublin. They organize one of the most exciting events of the year, the St Patrick's Day Parade (see page 38).

▲ New Yorkers from many backgrounds live side by side. Here all kinds of people mingle at Coney Island Beach (see page 17).

Little Italy

Thousands of Italians emigrated to New York from the late 19th century. Most settled in Manhattan's Lower East Side, in an area that became known as Little Italy. There they lived in crowded **tenements**, opened Italian restaurants and held Italian festivals. Now most New York Italians live in the Belmont area of the Bronx, but Little Italy has kept its unique style.

New York's Jews

Jews moved into the Lower East Side at about the same time as Italians. There they built synagogues (places of worship) and opened shops selling **kosher** food. Many Jews still live in the area, but others have moved out of Manhattan. There is now a large community of **Hasidic Jews** in the Crown Heights area of Brooklyn.

◄ **Orthodox** Jews stroll through Chinatown. The boy in the front of the picture wears the traditional Jewish *yarmulke* (skullcap).

Chinatown

Many Chinese men first went to the USA to find work mining gold and building railroads. By the 1880s about 10,000 had moved to New York. Most lived in the Chinatown area of the Lower East Side, to the south of Little Italy. Now over 200,000 Chinese people live there. Its streets are lined with restaurants (see page 33) as well as antique shops, Chinese medicine centres and **Buddhist** temples (see page 23).

▲ Shoppers in New York's Chinatown. Food stores in this area sell all kinds of ingredients for Chinese cooking, for example noodles and bamboo shoots.

PUERTO RICANS

About a quarter of New Yorkers are **Latinos**. Many came from Puerto Rico, a Caribbean island that has been part of the USA since 1899. During the 1950s, the US government encouraged Puerto Ricans to move to New York. Some settled in the south-east of Harlem, known as Spanish Harlem or El Barrio. Others moved into Manhattan's West Side. Gang warfare there between Puerto Ricans and non-Puerto Ricans inspired the musical *West Side Story* by Leonard Bernstein.

African-Americans

African-Americans have lived in New York since its early years, when many were slaves. After the city abolished slavery in 1827, more moved there from the South, where slavery was still allowed. Even more made the journey north during the **Second World War**. By the 1950s about one million black people lived in the area of Harlem, very often in poor slum housing. Since the 1970s the situation has improved, but many black New Yorkers have moved away to areas such as the Bronx.

African-Americans form about 30 per cent ▲ of the New York population and make a vital contribution to the life of the city.

The most famous buildings in New York are the gleaming skyscrapers that soar high above the streets of Manhattan. The city also has 65 bridges that link the city's islands to the mainland and each other.

The Flatiron Building

The first real skyscraper in New York was the Flatiron Building at Fifth Avenue and 23rd Street. This steel-framed, stone-covered structure was completed in 1902 and is shaped like a long, narrow triangle. It was given its name because many people thought that it looked like an iron. Others think that it is more like the bow (front) of a ship. The building rises 87 metres above the ground and has 21 storeys.

▲ The strange shape of the Flatiron Building (left) makes the wind rush along the streets below. The spire of the Chrysler Building (right) is made of gleaming stainless steel.

◄ The Federal Hall National Memorial stands on the site where **George Washington** was sworn in as president (see page 9). At the entrance is a statue of the great man.

The Chrysler Building

The Chrysler Building was built for Walter Chrysler, owner of the Chrysler motor car company. Architect William Van Alen designed this 77-storey **Art Deco** masterpiece and used a car theme for many of its special features – for example, its eagle decorations are based on car bonnet mascots. When the 319-metre-high skyscraper was finished in 1930, it was the world's tallest building.

The Empire State Building

In 1931 the new, 381-metre-tall Empire State Building beat the Chrysler's height record. This 102-storey skyscraper was built at the rate of over four storeys each week. Sandwich stands were set up on several floors so that workers did not waste time going down to the street to buy food. In 1945 an American bomber flew into the building. Fourteen people were killed, but the skyscraper stayed upright.

The World Trade Centre

In 1973 the 110-storey World Trade Centre took over from the Empire State as New York's highest building. One of its twin towers was 416 metres tall, the other a metre shorter. In 1993, a terrorist bomb exploded in a car park underneath the building, killing six people (see page 27), and in 2001 a terrorist attack destroyed both towers (see page 11). A permanent memorial is now planned for the site (see page 42).

GRAND CENTRAL TERMINAL

Grand Central Terminal (below) is not only a busy railway station (see page 29) but also a stunning **Beaux-Arts** building. The huge stone and marble structure opened in 1913. Among its magnificent features are a sweeping staircase and a giant, sculpture-covered clock. The terminal was made a protected National Landmark in 1978 and has recently been restored to its original glory. The ceiling was cleaned so that the design of zodiac signs and 2,500 stars on a bright blue background can be clearly seen.

▲ People crossing Brooklyn Bridge. This picture also shows the World Trade Centre (the two tall towers on the left) before its destruction.

Brooklyn Bridge

The 486-metre-long Brooklyn Bridge spans East River, linking Brooklyn and Manhattan. Its architect, John Roebling, died before construction began. His son, Washington, got the **bends** after working on the project under water and was paralysed. Accidents killed 20 builders and, after the bridge opened in 1883, 12 people died in a stampede. Now the tragic past is largely forgotten and the bridge is admired for its beauty.

OPEN SPACES

Early city planners did not think that New York needed many parks. They believed that enough fresh air blew in from the sea to keep people healthy and happy. Yet now the city has over 20,000 hectares of parkland.

Central Park

Until the mid-19th century much of central Manhattan was home to farming settlements and other small communities. Then newspaper editor William Cullen Bryant persuaded city leaders to turn the area into a park. Central Park, as it became, was designed by Frederick Law Olmsted (see page 40) and Calvert Vaux. Now its 340 hectares contain half a million trees, several lakes, a roller-skating rink, a theatre, the Metropolitan Museum of Art (see page 36) and much more.

▲ Many New Yorkers enjoy jogging, cycling or rollerblading in Central Park. Others prefer a stroll around its wide green spaces – with or without their pets.

▲ Castle Clinton now stands in Battery Park. The park is named after the **battery** of cannons that the castle once contained.

Battery Park

Another large green space in Manhattan was created during the 1980s. Battery Park is on the borough's southern tip. It was built on rubble dug up during construction of the World Trade Centre (see page 15). The rubble was also used to link the mainland to Castle Clinton, which stood in the Hudson River. The castle was first a fort, then the place where **immigrants** arrived before the Ellis Island complex opened (see page 37).

Flushing Meadows-Corona Park

The borough of Queens contains the Flushing Meadows-Corona Park, which covers 500 hectares. The park is best known as the home of the US Open Tennis Championships (see page 39). It also contains the Unisphere, a giant steel ball that weighs over 300,000 kg and was originally built for a fair in 1964. The park houses a wildlife centre, too, devoted to North American animals.

Daring acrobats entertain the ➤ crowds in Washington Square, at the heart of fashionable Greenwich Village (see page 19).

Bronx Zoo

Bronx Zoo, the biggest in New York, is home to about 4,000 animals and 500 birds. Many are kept in open areas similar to their natural habitats. For example, rainforest creatures roam the Jungle World exhibit, while mountain animals, such as snow leopards, live in a mini-Himalayas. There is also a children's zoo, where young visitors can enjoy activities such as climbing up artificial spiders' webs.

New York Botanical Garden

Just north of the Bronx Zoo is the New York **Botanical Garden**. Its features include a huge glass conservatory with a crystal dome. Inside there are many exotic plants, such as palms, as well as a desert area. The city has several other botanical gardens, including one in Brooklyn which includes a collection of bonsai trees and a Japanese garden.

ON THE BEACH

There are beaches in many parts of New York. One of the most popular is Coney Island Beach in Brooklyn. Visitors there can swim in the sea, enjoy the amusement park (left), eat hot dogs and visit the New York Aquarium, which contains about 10,000 fish. Further afield is the Rockaways, a finger of land that juts out into the Atlantic Ocean. Here the waves are strong enough for surfing.

HOMES AND HOUSING

The people of New York have always included both rich and poor. The wide variety of housing in the city reflects the huge differences in wealth of its inhabitants.

Tenements and projects

From about 1850, builders began to construct brick **tenements** as homes for **immigrants** in the Lower East Side (see page 12). The flats were cramped and unhygienic and **tuberculosis** quickly spread. Tenement designs were later improved, but the blocks are still slums, many of them lived in by Puerto Rican immigrants. Thousands of poor New Yorkers also live in **housing projects**, for example in Harlem.

▲ During the 19th century, Little Italy was full of new immigrants. Large families lived in tiny flats and some people opened shops below.

▼ In 1867 the New York authorities passed a law requiring all tenement blocks to have fire escapes. These metal stairs still exist.

Row houses

As poor immigrants moved into southern Manhattan, middle-class families moved north. Land was expensive because it was scarce, so many people bought or built row (terraced) houses rather than wide, detached homes. Many row houses were brownstones, so called because they were made of red-brown sandstone. These homes, in areas such as Chelsea, are still very popular.

Millionaires' mansions

New York's richest 19th-century citizens did not have to worry about the cost of housing. They built mansions in fashionable areas such as Fifth Avenue, east of Central Park. This is still one of the city's most chic addresses, but there are now more apartments than mansions. There are also many expensive homes west of Central Park, especially along Riverside Drive.

▲ Typical New York brownstones. Each house has a stoop – a small flight of steps outside that leads to a doorstep platform.

THE DAKOTA BUILDING

The Dakota apartment building stands on 72nd Street, just west of Central Park. When it opened in 1884 it was the first luxury housing in the area. Many famous people have lived there over the years. They include the pop star John Lennon, who was shot dead outside the building in 1980. Lennon's widow, Yoko Ono, still lives in the Dakota. She created the Strawberry Fields garden in Central Park, opposite the building, as a memorial to her husband.

SoHo and TriBeCa

SoHo, the district *So*uth of *Ho*uston Street in Manhattan, was once an industrial area. Now it is home to artists and others who moved in when housing in nearby Greenwich Village became too expensive. Since the 1960s many people have converted SoHo warehouses into **loft flats**. Others have moved into the area's 19th-century houses with cast-iron fronts. Now SoHo is expensive, so people are moving to nearby TriBeCa, the *Tri*angle *Be*low *Ca*nal Street, and making new lofts there.

Battery Park City

Battery Park City lies next to Battery Park (see page 16) and was also built on rubble from the World Trade Centre site. Builders have constructed several expensive apartment blocks, both low- and high-rise, in the nine-hectare area. Residents can enjoy many new facilities, including a walkway along the Hudson River lined with trees and ponds.

▲ In the 19th and early 20th centuries Greenwich Village was a rich, quiet suburb. The beautiful homes of Grove Court are among many remaining from that era.

EDUCATION

The New York authorities encourage learning for people of all ages and run thousands of schools and colleges. The city also provides private education.

Public and private

Before the mid-19th century, many children in the USA received little or no education. Most of those who did go to school went to private, church or charity institutions. Then, in 1853, free, public education for all children began in New York City. Private education still exists, but it is far less common.

School system

American children must complete 12 years of education. In New York City this lasts from the ages of 6 to 17. Children begin at elementary school, move on to middle school and finish at high school, where most gain a diploma. Many parents now start their children's schooling early by sending them to kindergartens.

▲ A typical New York City school playground. The wall next to the school has been decorated with brightly coloured murals.

Local school boards

The New York Board of Education is in overall charge of public schooling in the city, but local school boards run its elementary and middle schools on a day-to-day basis. They have to deal with different conditions in different areas. In poor districts, they may have to work for better school buildings. In areas with many **immigrants** they may have to employ staff to teach pupils English.

◀ Special buses like this take many New York children safely to their schools in the morning and home again in the evening.

New York universities

New York has six main universities. The oldest, Columbia University in Manhattan, is private. It was founded in 1754 and belongs to the **Ivy League**. For many years, only men could study there, while women went to Barnard College nearby. Since 1983 the university has been for both men and women. New York University, in Greenwich Village, is the largest private university in the USA, while the large City University of New York is publicly funded.

▲ The buildings of Columbia University are on the Upper West Side. They include the domed Low Memorial Library (above).

THE SCHOMBURG CENTRE

The Schomburg Centre for Research in Black Culture lies in the centre of Harlem. It contains the world's biggest collection of books, films and other material about the history of black people in the USA and their present-day ways of life. There are about five million items in all, some on display in the Centre's museum, others in its library. The Centre is used by scholars and other visitors who value this unique place to study.

Specialist education

New York offers a variety of high schools for pupils who want to specialize from their teenage years, for example the School of the Performing Arts. There are also many specialist higher education centres. Rockefeller University is the place for scientific and medical research. The Juilliard School in the Lincoln Centre (see page 34) is where musicians, dancers and actors learn their skills.

◀ The Juilliard School is named after Augustus D Juilliard, who in the 1920s left money in his will to set it up.

RELIGION

Most New Yorkers are Christians, but the city is also home to a large Jewish population, as well as Muslims and **Buddhists**.

Early churches

Many of the first Europeans in New York were **Protestant** Christians. In 1654, when the city was still New Amsterdam (see page 8), a Protestant church was built in Flatbush, Brooklyn. A later church now stands there, but old Dutch graves remain in the cemetery. Another early church was Trinity Church, which opened in Manhattan in 1846.

▲ A gospel choir made up of men, women and children sings at a service in a church in Harlem.

Protestantism today

Now more than ten per cent of New Yorkers are **Baptists**. Many of these are African-Americans who attend churches in Harlem, famous for their stirring **gospel** choirs. Many other Protestants belong to the **Episcopal Church**. Their biggest place of worship is the Cathedral of St John the Divine. Construction of the church began in 1892 and will not end before 2050. When it does, the cathedral will be the world's largest.

Roman Catholicism

Roman Catholicism is the religion of more New Yorkers than any other – over 43 per cent of the city's population are members. Many belong to families that originally came from Ireland or Italy, where Catholicism is the main faith. The most important Catholic church in New York, and the largest in the USA, is St Patrick's Cathedral on Fifth Avenue, Manhattan. It was completed in 1879.

Judaism

The first group of Jews to settle in New York – there were just 23 – arrived from Brazil in 1654. The Jewish community grew slowly until the late 19th century, when immigration soared (see page 10). Now about 11 per cent of New Yorkers are Jewish. Some belong to the **Orthodox** branch of Judaism, others to a more liberal tradition. Major Jewish places of worship in the city are Temple Emanu-El on Fifth Avenue and the Eldridge Street Synagogue on the Lower East Side.

Islam

There are thousands of Muslims in New York. Some are native New Yorkers, others come from all around the world. The city contains many mosques (places of worship), including some for particular Islamic groups, for example the Turkish community. The most important mosque in the city is in Manhattan's Islamic Cultural Centre. An Islamic school is now being built there too.

▲ All mosques must point towards Mecca, where Mohammed, the founder of Islam, was born. The correct position for New York's Islamic Cultural Centre was worked out by computer.

◄ St Patrick's Cathedral was designed by architect James Renwick. When it was built in the 19th century, it stood on the edge of New York City. Now it is in the centre.

BUDDHA AND CONFUCIUS

Many members of New York's Chinese community are Buddhists. There are 12 Buddhist temples in Manhattan's Chinatown, including this one (left). Some Chinese people follow the teachings of Confucius. A bronze statue of this wise man, who lived in China from 551 to 479 BC, stands in Chinatown, on the edge of Confucius Plaza.

INDUSTRY AND FINANCE

New York has many factories and banks, as well as tourist and media industries. But economic uncertainty caused by the events of 11 September, 2001 (see page 11) has led to the loss of over 100,000 jobs in the city.

Docks in decline

New York was once the USA's busiest port. By the 1890s huge amounts of American produce were being brought along railways, the Erie Canal and the Hudson River to its docks for transport abroad. Some cargo ships still sail in and out of the city, but more use ports in nearby New Jersey, which have more modern facilities.

Huge sailing ships line the quayside at South Street (see page 37) in this busy scene from the 1870s.

The manufacturing industry

Thousands of 19th-century **immigrants** worked in New York's clothing factories, where conditions were often dangerous. In 1911 a fire at the Triangle Shirtwaist Factory killed 146 people, forcing the authorities to introduce safety laws. Clothing is still a big New York business, especially in Manhattan's Garment District. Another major industry is food-processing. But many companies have moved out of the city as rents and wages are so high.

◄ A Garment District worker wheels a rack of new clothes from a factory to a nearby warehouse. About 200,000 people work in the Garment District.

TOURIST TRADE

About 30 million tourists visit New York each year, over five million of them from abroad. A wealthy few still sail in on luxury liners, but most arrive by air. The tourist trade provides work for thousands of New Yorkers, for example as tour guides showing people around the city, as well as in travel agencies, restaurants, hotels, museums and theatres.

The Financial District

New York's Financial District covers the southern tip of Manhattan. The New York Stock Exchange, on Wall Street, is at its heart. It was set up in 1792 and people have bought and sold shares there ever since. The **Wall Street Crash** of 1929 (see page 11) led to serious losses. One of the US government's main banks stands nearby. It contains 11,000 tonnes of gold bars, so security is very tight.

Banks and businesses

There are many other banks and businesses in the Financial District. Some are in the World Finance Centre, while others, such as the mighty Chase Manhattan Bank, have their own, specially designed headquarters. There are major companies in Midtown Manhattan, too, especially in the Rockefeller Centre. But the many businesses once based in the World Trade Centre have had to find alternative accommodation.

▲ There are 21 separate buildings in the giant Rockefeller Centre. Towering over them all is the 259-metre-high General Electric Building, containing the offices of many different companies.

Media world

Book, newspaper and magazine publishing is an important New York industry. Much of this is based in Midtown Manhattan. Newspapers include the *New York Times* and *The Wall Street Journal*. Many TV and radio stations have bases in the city. They include the National Broadcasting Company (NBC), which has studios in the Rockefeller Centre. Top advertising agencies can be found on Madison Avenue.

The Wall Street Journal is essential reading ➤ for people who want to follow the rise and fall of their shares as well as the latest news.

New York was once famous for its high levels of crime, including murder. They have been declining since the early 1990s under Mayor David Dinkins, and later Mayor Rudolph Giuliani (see page 41). But the city still has problems.

The NYPD

The New York Police Department (NYPD) fights crime across the city. New York has 76 police districts, each with its own commander, officers and station. The city's Police Headquarters is on Police Plaza, near City Hall. NYPD officers wear blue trousers, shirts and ties and a peaked cap with a gold badge. All are armed with guns. Unofficial law enforcers called Guardian Angels try to assist the police by patrolling streets and subways.

▲ William Marcy 'Boss' Tweed was a 19th-century leader of the New York Democratic Party. He took bribes and stole city funds worth $200 million, but was later imprisoned and died in jail.

▲ Both men and women serve in the NYPD. The force's badge appears on their shirt sleeves and on the official cars they drive.

Cracking crime

The police work to beat crime in many ways. For example, Street Crimes Units patrol dangerous areas such as the Bronx. Details of crimes are fed into computers then analysed to work out when and where criminals are likely to strike again. Since the introduction of these and other tactics, crimes have decreased. The number of murders has gone down by about 70 per cent.

PROHIBITION

In 1920 the US government banned the manufacture and sale of alcohol and the **Prohibition** era began. Thousands of people in New York, as elsewhere in the country, did not obey the new laws. Criminals called **bootleggers** produced and sold alcohol illegally. Other people set up clubs called speakeasies where customers bought alcohol (right). During the **depression** that followed the **Wall Street Crash** (see page 11), the government needed to find jobs for people wherever it could, even in alcohol manufacturing. So, in 1933, it abolished Prohibition.

City crimes

Even after the recent improvements, some crimes still occur regularly in New York. Among them are pickpocketing, mugging and car theft. Illegal drug use is also common. Gang warfare is another problem. In Chinatown groups known as Tongs often clash. Racial violence sometimes flares up, too, for example between the black and Jewish communities in Crown Heights, Brooklyn (see page 12).

▲ New York's police and medical services come to the rescue of a person injured during the 1997 shooting at the Empire State Building.

High-profile crimes

As well as common offences, major, high-profile crimes sometimes happen in New York. In 1997, a gunman killed one tourist and injured seven others at the top of the Empire State Building. The World Trade Centre was the target of terrorist attacks in February 1993 and, far more devastatingly, in September 2001 (see pages 11 and 15).

Going to Court

There are many courts in New York City. Some try people for crimes against federal (national) laws, others for crimes against state laws. Several of them – including the US Courthouse and the Criminal Courts Building – stand in Manhattan's Civic Center. New York's average prison population is over 18,000.

GETTING AROUND

New Yorkers seem to be always on the move. In Manhattan the pavements are full of scurrying pedestrians, while cars, buses and taxis jam the roads. Subway trains are packed and even harbours are busy as ferries sail in and out.

On the road

Driving in central New York is only for the daring, so people often take one of the famous yellow taxis instead. There are about 12,000 of them in the city. Many are driven by new **immigrants**, some of whom do not know the language or the layout of New York very well. Another way to get around overground is to take a bus. Two hundred routes cross the city, but buses, like cars, are often stuck in traffic. Long-distance buses run from the Port Authority Bus Terminal in Manhattan.

▲ Yellow taxis and private cars move bumper to bumper along the six lanes of Manhattan's busy 42nd Street.

Subway system

New York's first subway (underground) line opened in 1904. Now the system has 469 stations and is used by over three million people every day. There are two types of subway train. Local trains stop at every station. Express trains go faster and miss out some stations. The subway was once dirty and dangerous. Now stations and trains have been cleaned and improved, but travelling at night can still be risky.

◄ New York's express buses do not make many stops, so they go much faster than regular buses – but they still cannot avoid the jams.

Rail travel

Manhattan has four main railway stations. Trains on an amazing 123 lines run in and out of Grand Central Terminal (see page 15). Local trains to New Jersey use the stations on Sixth Avenue and at the World Trade Centre. Penn (Pennsylvania) Station is a terminus for both commuter services and long-distance trains.

▲ A train waits at a Grand Central Terminal platform. Most trains from this station carry workers in and out of New York every day.

FULL STEAM AHEAD

In 1807 American engineer Robert Fulton launched the *Clermont*, a **paddle-wheel steamboat**, in New York City. It made its way up the Hudson River to Albany in just 32 hours – three times faster than sailing boats. Soon this fast method of transport was being used to carry goods from inland and western areas to New York. This was one reason why the city became a major port (see page 24).

On the water

New York can easily be explored by water. Regular ferries take passengers from Battery Park to the Statue of Liberty, providing them with superb views of Manhattan. The ferries also visit Ellis Island (see page 37). Longer cruises are available on boats and catamarans. The luxurious *QE2* liner begins and ends its journeys at New York's Passenger Ship Terminal.

Air travel

New York has three major airports. The main international airport is John F Kennedy (JFK), in the borough of Queens. Flights to and from other parts of the USA fly in and out of La Guardia Airport, also in Queens. Newark Airport in New Jersey is used for international and internal travel. Helicopter sightseeing trips fly from three Manhattan heliports.

▲ The Staten Island Ferry, which travels from Manhattan to the island, is free and operates 24 hours a day. It is used by tourists and working New Yorkers alike.

SHOPS AND MARKETS

New York City, especially Manhattan, is a shopper's paradise. But buyers must beware – after a day's serious spending, their bags will be full but their wallets will be empty and their feet sore.

Department stores

There are over 30 department stores in New York. Among them is Macy's, the world's largest. It opened on Broadway in 1858, where it still stands. Clothes, cosmetics and other goods are sold on its ten floors. The famous Bloomingdale's store sells a wide range of goods, including clothing and gourmet foods. These old-established American shops have now been joined by a Japanese rival, Takashimaya.

Fine fashions

Many New York stores specialize in clothes. Designers such as Christian Dior have shops on and around Fifth and Madison Avenues. SoHo is the place to buy more unusual outfits. The city also has many vintage clothing stores. They include Fan Club, where buyers may find dresses worn by stars such as Marilyn Monroe.

▲ Thousands of people flood through the doors of Macy's department store every day. If they grow tired of shopping, they can eat there, too.

Diamond-dealing

People looking for jewellery to go with their high-fashion clothes are spoilt for choice in New York. They can head for specialist stores such as Cartier and Tiffany's on Fifth Avenue. Or they can go to Manhattan's Diamond District and deal direct with gem, gold and silver traders, as well as independent jewellers. Experts are also on hand to string their precious purchases to make unique necklaces and bracelets.

◄ Chic clothes in the windows of Bergdorf Goodman's Fifth Avenue store are designed to attract wealthy shoppers.

Children's choice

Children can find plenty of places to spend their money in New York, too. They include the FAO Schwarz toy store on Fifth Avenue, one of the world's biggest toy shops. At the entrance there is a singing clock and an actor dressed as a toy soldier who greets visitors. Inside, staff demonstrate many of the games and toys for sale. Niketown is another store that is popular with children. It sells all sorts of stylish sportswear.

▲ A jewellery store in 47th Street, known as Diamond Row. Many of the traders are Jews who had to leave their diamond businesses in Holland before the **Second World War**.

▲ This New York florist has created a spectacular autumn display, mixing vibrant orange pumpkins with bright red and yellow flowers.

NEW YORK MARKETS

There are many types of market in New York. The Annex on Sixth Avenue is one of the best **flea markets**. It is held at weekends and items for sale on its 600 stalls include antiques. **Greenmarkets** are very popular. One of the biggest takes place on Union Square, where farmers sell fresh produce and home-cooked foods such as herbs, honey and **pretzels**. Manhattan's main flower market is on Sixth Avenue, but not all the plants on show are for sale to the public. Many are bought by professional florists, who use them to decorate grand homes and offices.

Book-buying

Adults and children alike can enjoy browsing in New York's 500 or more book shops. Barnes & Noble stores are all around the city and provide people with sofas to sit on while they make their choice. They can spend hours if necessary, as the shops are open until midnight. Strand Book Store on Broadway is the largest second-hand book shop in the USA. It stocks about two million different titles.

FOOD AND DRINK

New Yorkers love their food and the city's 17,000 restaurants do a roaring trade. Thanks to the many **immigrant** communities, there is a huge variety of cooking. Everything from Jewish **bagels** to Japanese **sushi** can be found here.

Eating out

Hard-working New Yorkers are always in a hurry and many people eat out more often than at home. The day often starts with breakfast at a diner. This might be **eggs sunny side up** with bacon, waffles or syrup-drenched pancakes, juice and coffee, or just a Danish pastry with coffee. Lunch is generally a **deli** sandwich or some other fast food. At dinner the serious eating begins.

▲ This fish shop in Chinatown sells all kinds of fresh seafood. Many of the items here are sold to local restaurants.

American dishes

Food from all over the Americas is available in New York. One of the most famous restaurants serving traditional North American dishes, such as meatloaf, is the Empire Diner in Chelsea. Sylvia's in Harlem offers food from the American South, such as fried chicken. During the mid-morning **Gospel** Brunch, a choir sings while customers eat.

TOP FOOD SHOPS

New York has many fine food stores. Two of the most famous are on Broadway – Zabar's, known for its Jewish delicacies such as lox (smoked salmon), and Dean and Deluca which features Italian and other specialities. Balducci's food store, in Greenwich Village, grew from a street stall to a huge shop. Street food stalls are also popular, such as this one selling Jewish-style pickles (left).

Ethnic cooking

Jewish food is extremely popular in New York. It can be enjoyed at places such as Yonah Schimmel's, which specializes in bagels and stuffed pastries called **knishes**. Italian cooking is also a favourite. There are many Italian restaurants in Little Italy (see page 12) and John's in Greenwich Village makes some of the best pizzas in the city. A huge variety of Chinese food is available in Chinatown, from steamed dumplings to crispy duck.

▼ This grand steak restaurant is one of a chain owned by the baseball star Michael Jordan. It stands inside Grand Central Terminal (see page 15).

Expensive eating

New York also offers ultra-expensive restaurants, some more famous for their customers than their cooking. Top spots include Elaine's, a favourite of Woody Allen's (see page 41), and the Four Seasons, where paintings by Picasso decorate the walls. The Peter Luger restaurant on Broadway specializes in steak, as it has done since it opened in 1887.

Fast food

New York contains every kind of traditional fast food outlet, from hamburger restaurants to hot dog stands. But there is more on offer, too. Delis will make almost any kind of sandwich – a New York favourite is pastrami (smoked, spiced beef) on rye bread. Cafés serve drinks, snacks and cakes, including cheesecake, a speciality of the city.

◀ Sausages, hot dogs, *knishes*, **pretzels** and soft drinks are all for sale at this New York fast food stall.

ENTERTAINMENT

The New York entertainment scene is among the best in the world, offering everything from serious theatre and opera to popular films and baseball games.

Broadway and beyond

The area around Times Square is the centre of New York's Theatre District. It is known as Broadway, but also includes other streets nearby. There are about 30 Broadway theatres, which stage popular musicals and comedies. Serious works are often produced at smaller **Off-Broadway** venues such as the Joseph Papp Public Theater. It is owned by the city authorities and runs an annual Shakespeare Festival. Even smaller, Off-Off-Broadway theatres also put on shows.

▲ The Radio City Music Hall stands near the Rockefeller Centre. Since the 1930s many famous stars have performed there.

Movie mania

Many big New York movie theatres (cinemas) are in the Times Square district. There are also multi-screen venues elsewhere, for example on Third Avenue. Some movie theatres specialize in classic American films or films from abroad. The new Walter E. Reade Theatre in the Lincoln Centre (see below) shows both. New York's main Imax cinema is part of a Broadway multiplex.

▼ Dancers from the Alvin Ailey American Dance Theatre performing at City Centre, a popular modern dance venue.

Classical music

One of the main venues for classical music is the Lincoln Centre on the Upper West Side. Buildings that make up the Centre include the Metropolitan Opera House, the New York State Theatre, where the New York Opera and New York Ballet perform, and the Avery Fisher Hall, home of the New York Philharmonic Orchestra.

Jazz and rock

New York caters for fans of many other types of music, too. Jazz-lovers can take their pick from several top clubs in the city. Among the most famous are the Village Vanguard, which dates from 1935, and the Blue Note. Both are in Greenwich Village. Major rock stadiums include Madison Square Garden, which can house an audience of about 20,000.

Sports scene

New Yorkers love to participate in sport, if only by jogging around Central Park. They also support their professional teams. The city's most successful baseball team are the New York Yankees, who play at Yankee Stadium in the Bronx. The New York Mets, whose home is Shea Stadium in Queens, have many followers too. Thousands of basketball fans support the New York Knicks (Knickerbockers), based at Madison Square Garden. This is also a venue for major boxing contests.

THE HARLEM RENAISSANCE

An important black cultural movement emerged in Harlem in the 1920s. Poets such as Langston Hughes, novelists such as Zora Neale Hurston and artists such as Archibald Motley were all members. But now people are more likely to remember the entertainers, such as jazz pianist and composer Duke Ellington and band leader Cab Calloway. Both played at the famous Cotton Club (above). Jazz singer Billie Holiday also began her career in the clubs of Harlem.

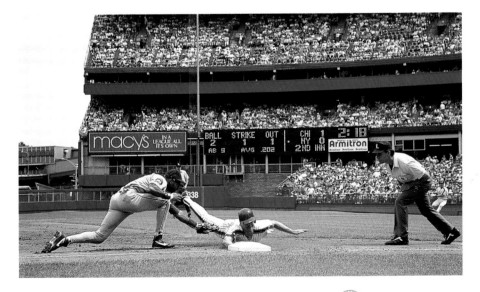

◄ The New York Mets in action at Shea Stadium. A huge crowd follows the game and cheers on the team.

MUSEUMS AND GALLERIES

There are over 150 museums in New York, including several that contain major art collections. The city also has about 500 private galleries, showing a wide variety of works.

▲ The Met contains more than 300 exhibition rooms, some of which house temporary displays. Banners outside announce these shows.

The Metropolitan Museum of Art

The 250-room Metropolitan Museum of Art (the Met) contains over three million objects. These include paintings by many of the world's finest artists, for example Rembrandt and Van Gogh, as well as precious ancient objects from around the world. The Met also contains a complete building, the Ancient Egyptian Temple of Dendur.

MOMA

The Museum of Modern Art (MOMA) has a stunning collection, but none of its 100,000 treasures dates from before 1880. The museum contains works by artists such as Monet, Picasso and New Yorker Andy Warhol. One of Warhol's famous pictures of Marilyn Monroe hangs here. The museum also displays photographs, sculpture and more.

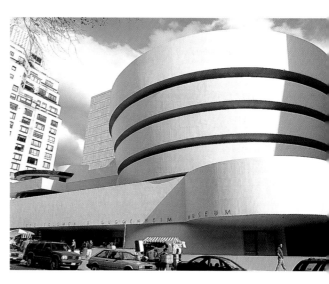

The Guggenheim Museum

The huge white whorl of the Guggenheim Museum (1959) was designed by American architect Frank Lloyd Wright, and is itself worth a close look. The museum was built to hold the art collection of its rich founder, Solomon R Guggenheim. It contains works by famous modern artists such as Paul Klee and Vasili Kandinsky.

▲ The Guggenheim Museum's spiral shape has earned it the nickname 'The Big Seashell'. There is another, smaller, Guggenheim in the SoHo area.

South Street Seaport

An exciting place to visit on the East River bank is the South Street Seaport Historical District. The South Street Docks were once New York's busiest, but by the mid-20th century were in a state of disrepair. Developers have now renovated the area. There are large ships and a museum to explore and visitors can even take a trip on a sailing ship.

▲ The contrast between old and new can clearly be seen at South Street Seaport where modern skyscrapers tower over 19th-century ships.

The American Museum of Natural History

Packed with 36 million items, this is the largest natural history museum in the world and probably the largest museum of any kind. The dinosaur display has some of the most exciting exhibits, but there is much more to see, including a 29-metre-long blue whale and the Star of India, the biggest blue sapphire ever found. The museum also has a **planetarium**.

The Intrepid Sea-Air-Space Museum

Floating on the Hudson River, alongside Pier 86, is an old US Navy aircraft carrier called the *Intrepid*. Visitors can climb aboard to view jet fighters, spy planes and many other exhibits that tell the story of warfare at sea and in the air, as well as the history of sea and space exploration. There is also a submarine next to the ship that people can look inside.

ELLIS ISLAND

From 1892 all **immigrants** who arrived in New York had to disembark at Ellis Island, where they were registered and examined by doctors. They also had to answer questions about their political beliefs. More than 12 million people had passed through the island by 1954, when it was abandoned. In 1990 its buildings were re-opened as an Immigration Museum (left). Visitors follow the path immigrants took and hear recordings of their moving stories.

New Yorkers never have a reason to be bored. There is something to do all year round, from the depths of winter to the height of summer.

Warming up

There are several ways for people to take their minds off the freezing temperatures of January and February. They can head to Chinatown to watch, or join in, celebrations for Chinese New Year. The festivities include dragon dances and exploding firecrackers. In February, any New Yorkers with enough stamina can do the Empire State Building Run-Up. Climbing the 1,860 steps in a few minutes keeps out the cold.

▲ Young Irish dancers in traditional embroidered costumes take part in the lively St Patrick's Day Parade.

Spring parades

The big event of early spring is the St Patrick's Day Parade on the weekend nearest to 17 March. St Patrick is the **patron saint** of Ireland and the Irish community celebrates in style. Thousands of people march through the city and bands play rousing Irish music. At Easter there is a parade from Central Park to the Rockefeller Centre, in which women traditionally wear flowery bonnets.

▲ Spectacular fireworks explode high above New York during Independence Day festivities.

Sporting season

As the weather improves, the number of sporting events grows. The baseball season begins in April and in May the Great Five Borough Bike Tour takes place. Thousands of people complete the 68-kilometre-long course. 17 May is Martin Luther King Memorial Day, when a parade commemorates the work of this great activist for black **civil rights**.

Summer highlight

The highlight of summer is the celebration on 4 July, Independence Day. This marks the date in 1776 when the USA declared its independence from Britain. The Stars and Stripes **Regatta** is held at South Street Seaport, Macy's department store stages a firework display and the New York Philharmonic Orchestra plays in Central Park.

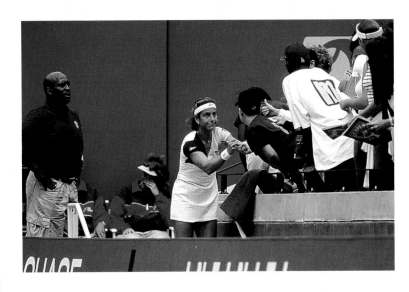

Autumn arrivals

In September both the US Open Tennis Championships and the New York Film Festival take place, the film festival continuing into October. On 12 October the Columbus Day Parade marks the 1492 arrival in the Americas of explorer Christopher Columbus. The New York Marathon is run in November, from Staten Island all the way to Central Park.

▲ Fans greet a player at the US Open Tennis Championships. During matches, planes are not allowed to fly overhead.

THANKSGIVING

Thanksgiving, on the last Thursday in November, is a time of great celebration throughout the USA. It marks the day in 1621 when the **Pilgrims** celebrated their first harvest in Massachusetts. In New York, Macy's store organizes a Thanksgiving Day Parade through the city. There are floats, bands and fun for everyone, especially children.

Christmas and Chanukah

At Christmas New York's streets are decorated and a huge tree is put up at the Metropolitan Museum of Art. The Jewish festival of Chanukah takes place at about the same time. A giant menorah (an eight-branched candlestick) stands on Fifth Avenue for its eight days. On 31 December people of all religions gather in Times Square to celebrate the New Year.

◄ Times Square at New Year. Thousands of people pack the square on New Year's Eve to join in the traditional countdown to midnight.

Over the years people with many skills have worked to make New York such a vibrant metropolis. Here you can read about a few of them.

Frederick Law Olmsted

American landscape designer Frederick Law Olmsted became superintendent of the future Central Park in 1857. The next year, with architect Calvert Vaux, he began work on his plan to create the park. He wanted it to be for the poor as well as the rich and to contain woods and lakes. He later designed other New York parks, such as Prospect Park in Brooklyn.

▲ Frederick Law Olmsted's aim in creating Central Park was to bring the countryside to the city. Many people think he succeeded.

Andrew Carnegie

Scotsman Andrew Carnegie arrived in the USA as a boy in 1848. He became a millionaire by working and investing in railways, oil and steel, then used his fortune to do good works – for example he made a donation of $125 million to set up the Carnegie Corporation of New York in 1911. Funds from this organization were used to improve the city. Some of the money paid for Carnegie Hall, still a major concert venue.

◄ Andrew Carnegie's first job was in a cotton mill, where he earned $1.20 a week. By 1905 he was rich enough to own the huge mansion in this picture.

Dorothy Parker

Dorothy Parker was born in New Jersey in 1893 but was educated in New York City. She became first a critic, working for magazines such as the *New Yorker*, then a poet and short-story writer. Dorothy Parker is remembered especially for her sharp wit. This was often on display at the Algonquin Round Table, a writers' group that met in New York's Algonquin Hotel during the 1920s and '30s.

▲ Dorothy Parker's work is still popular today. Many people visit the Algonquin Hotel on 44th Street to see where she and her friends met.

Woody Allen

Many people who have never visited New York have formed their idea of the city from the films of Woody Allen. Allen was born in Brooklyn in 1935. He made his first film in 1966 and rose to fame by writing, directing and starring in movies such as *Manhattan* (1979). He portrays New Yorkers, especially himself, as always worried about their lives and health. He now lives in the Upper East Side and is a keen supporter of the New York Knicks.

▲ One of Woody Allen's many talents is playing the clarinet. He often plays at Michael's Pub, a jazz club in central Manhattan.

▲ Rudolph Giuliani's first swearing-in ceremony as mayor of New York took place in January 1994. His family watched as he took the oath.

Rudolph Giuliani

Italian-American Rudolph (Rudy) Giuliani was born in Brooklyn in 1944. He studied at New York University Law School, then worked his way up to become US **Attorney** for the Southern District of New York in 1983. In 1993 he was elected **Republican** mayor of New York City and in 1997 won a second term. Giuliani guided New Yorkers through the grim aftermath of the 2001 terrorist attack (see page 11) with calm determination and a strong spirit.

THE FUTURE OF NEW YORK

In the 1990s New York City came out of a difficult time of rising crime and severe financial problems. But the tragedy of 11 September, 2001 (see page 11) has presented many new challanges.

▲ This model of Times Square was created by architects to show their plans for the clean-up of the area. Now most of their work is complete.

Cleaning up the city

In recent years much improvement work has been carried out in New York and more is under way. The Times Square area, which was once very sleazy, has been cleaned up and is now safer to visit at night. The American Museum of Natural History has been cleaned and its **planetarium** rebuilt. The Museum of Modern Art has been extended and the Reading Room of New York Public Library has been restored.

Building the future

New York has many new buildings and others still under construction. The Museum of Jewish Heritage in Battery Park City was completed in 1997. It tells the story of the **Holocaust** and is a six-sided shape like the Jewish **Star of David**. The New York authorities are now working with developers to decide what to build on 'Ground Zero', the 6.5-hectare site where the World Trade Centre once stood. Some people want only a quiet memorial plaza, park and museum. But others are keen to build shops and a 110-storey office block there, too.

▲ The Museum of Jewish Heritage shows pictures of some of the Jews who died in **concentration camps** during the **Second World War**.

Improving areas

The Bronx, with its high crime and poor housing, was for many years one of New York's biggest problems. Then, in 1991, local people began a project to improve their area. Now derelict homes have been renovated and businesses that had left are returning. People are even talking about the 'Bronx Miracle'. Similar improvements have been made in run-down parts of Harlem, where 35,000 new homes are being built.

◄ Site workers cleared about 1.5 million tonnes of debris from Ground Zero. On 30 May 2002 the recovery process was ended and a ceremony held for the workers and the victim's families.

Change ahead

Rudolph Giuliani (see page 41) hoped to become US **Senator** for New York State, but ill health forced him to withdraw from the election. Instead Hillary Clinton, a **Democrat** and wife of former US president Bill Clinton, became Senator on 7 November 2000. On 6 November 2001, a new mayor was elected, Michael Bloomberg, a republican media tycoon. So with City and state in new hands, there is likely to be change ahead.

▲ Hillary Clinton moved to New York from Washington DC so that she could campaign for the state elections more easily.

TIMELINE

This timeline shows some of the most important dates in the history of New York. All the events are mentioned earlier in the book.

PRE-16TH CENTURY AD

*Native Americans of the **Algonquian** and **Iroquois** families inhabit the New York area*

16TH CENTURY

1524
Italian explorer Giovanni da Verrazzano becomes first European to see future site of New York

17TH CENTURY

1609
Henry Hudson lands on Manhattan Island and sails down the future Hudson River

1624
*Dutch West India Company sets up the **colony** of New Netherlands in the New York area*

1625
First Dutch families move to Manhattan Island and found the town of New Amsterdam

1626
Peter Minuit becomes governor of New Amsterdam and buys it from Native Americans

1646
Peter Stuyvesant becomes governor of New Amsterdam

1653
Stuyvesant makes New Amsterdam a city

1664
British seize New Amsterdam and rename it New York

18TH CENTURY

1754
Columbia University founded

1775-83
The American Revolution; the British lose their American colonies, including New York, and the USA is founded

1789
*New York becomes capital of the USA and **George Washington** is sworn in as the country's first president there*

1790
Philadelphia replaces New York as US capital

1792
New York Stock Exchange established

19TH CENTURY

1800
New York population reaches 79,000

1811
Grid map for New York produced by the city commissioners

1820s
Mass immigration into New York begins

1825
Erie Canal opens

1827
Slavery abolished in New York

1842
*Croton **Aqueduct** brings pure water to New York for the first time*

1846
Trinity Church opens in Manhattan

1853

Free, public education for all begins in city

1858

Central Park laid out

1861-65

American **Civil War** leads to fighting
and riots in New York

1879

St Patrick's Cathedral completed

1883

Brooklyn Bridge opens

1884

Dakota Building completed

1886

Statue of Liberty unveiled

1892

Construction of Cathedral of St John
the Divine begins
Ellis Island opens to receive **immigrants**

1898

Manhattan Island joins Queens, Brooklyn,
Staten Island and the Bronx to form Greater
New York, the modern city

20TH CENTURY

1902

Flatiron Building completed

1904

First New York subway opens

1911

146 people die in a fire at the Triangle
Shirtwaist Factory

1913

Grand Central Terminal opens

1920s

Era of the Harlem Renaissance

1920-33

Prohibition era; alcohol banned

1929

The **Wall Street Crash** leads to
economic **depression**

1930

Chrysler Building completed

1931

Empire State Building completed

1945

American bomber flies into Empire
State Building

1954

Ellis Island closes as immigrant centre

1959

Guggenheim Museum opens

1964

Harlem **race riots**

1973

World Trade Centre opens

1975

New York is declared bankrupt

1987

Another Wall Street Crash

1990

Ellis Island reopens as a museum

1991

Beginning of a successful project by
Bronx residents to improve their area

1993

Bombing of the World Trade Centre
Rudolph Giuliani elected mayor

1997

Rudolph Giuliani re-elected mayor
Museum of Jewish Heritage opens
Gunman kills one tourist and injures seven
others at the Empire State Building

21ST CENTURY

2000

Democrat Hillary Rodham Clinton elected US
Senator for New York State

2001

Terrorist attack destroys World Trade Centre
and leaves some 2800 people dead
Michael Bloomberg replaces Rudolph Giuliani
as mayor of New York City

GLOSSARY

Algonquian   Of or belonging to a group of Native American peoples, for example the Wappinger, whose members speak languages of the Algonquian family.

aqueduct   A large pipe for carrying water over a long distance.

Art Deco   A style of art and architecture that was popular during the 1920s and '30s. It featured strong geometrical and sometimes also symmetrical shapes.

Attorney   A lawyer who is allowed to represent clients in court and at other legal proceedings.

bagels   Chewy ring-shaped rolls, boiled then baked.

Baptists   Members of a Protestant Christian group that believes in baptizing people when they understand and accept the Christian faith, rather than as babies.

battery   A group of large guns, such as cannons.

Beaux-Arts   In the decorative style used in the Paris School of Fine Arts (Ecole des Beaux-Arts) in France.

bends   Serious breathing difficulties, muscle pains and other problems caused by a sudden lowering of air pressure around the body. It often occurs in divers who return to the surface too quickly.

bootlegger   A criminal who made and sold alcohol during Prohibition. Bootleggers were so called because former smugglers of illegal alcohol hid the bottles in their boot-tops.

botanical garden   A garden where plants are studied by scientists as well as grown for public enjoyment.

Buddhist   A member of a religion that began in India in about 500 BC. It is based on the teaching of a prince called Gautama Siddhartha. He was later given the title 'Buddha', which means 'enlightened one'.

civil rights   The rights of an individual, for example the right to freedom of speech, regardless of race or colour.

civil war   A war between different groups within a country rather than between separate countries.

colony   A country that is occupied and ruled by the people of another country.

concentration camp   A camp where large numbers of people are held prisoner. In the Second World War the German Nazi Party set up camps where they killed over six million people, many of them Jews.

deli   A shop where speciality foods and sandwiches are sold. The word is short for 'delicatessen'.

Democrat   A member of the Democratic Party, one of the two main political parties in the USA. Democrats generally have more liberal views than Republicans.

depression   A time of low business growth, high unemployment and hardship.

eggs sunny side up   Fried eggs that are not turned during cooking, so that the whole, yellow yolk looks like the sun.

Episcopal Church   A branch of the Anglican Church, which also includes the Church of England.

flea market   A market that sells a wide variety of low-price, and sometimes second-hand, goods.

gospel   A type of Christian religious music that was first sung by black people in the southern USA.

Great Lakes   Five lakes on or near the border between the USA and Canada. They are: Superior, Huron, Erie, Ontario and Michigan.

greenmarket   A market to which country farmers bring meat, eggs, fruit, vegetables and other produce for sale.

Greenwich Mean Time   The time in Greenwich, England, which stands on the zero line of longitude. It is used as a base for calculating the time in the rest of the world.

Hasidic Jews   Members of a branch of Judaism (the Jewish religion) that began in 18th-century Poland. Hasidic men wear dark suits and hats.

Holocaust   The murder of millions of Jews and others by Germany's Nazi Party during the Second World War.

housing projects   Publicly funded housing developments designed for people who can afford only low rents.

immigrant   A person who comes to live in a country where he or she was not born and is not a citizen.

Iroquois   Of or belonging to a group of Native American peoples, for example the Mohawk, whose members speak languages of the Iroquoian family.

Ivy League   The eight most highly regarded universities in the USA. They include Harvard, Yale and Columbia.

knishes   Pastries stuffed with a filling such as potato or cheese. *Knishes* are a Jewish speciality.

kosher (of food)   Prepared according to Jewish religious laws.

Latinos   US citizens whose ancestors came from Spanish-speaking parts of South and Central America.

loft flats   Spacious, usually high-ceilinged flats on the top floor of a converted factory or warehouse.

longhouses   Houses of the type built by some Native American peoples. They were long and narrow with rounded roofs and were made of wooden poles covered with sheets of bark.

Off-Broadway   Of or relating to theatres that contain between 100 and 500 seats.

Orthodox   Of or relating to the branch of Judaism that strictly follows ancient beliefs and teachings.

paddle-wheel steamboat   A steam-driven boat with large wheels made of paddles (blades). The paddles are turned by the engine, making the boat move forward.

patron saint   A saint who is believed to protect and care for a particular place, organization or person.

Pilgrims   The group of English Puritans (strict Protestants) who arrived in Massachusetts, on North America's north-east coast, in 1620. They are also known as the Pilgrim Fathers.

planetarium   A building where images of the stars and planets are projected on to a dark ceiling.

pretzels   Hard, salty biscuits, often in the shape of knots.

Prohibition   The era (1920-1933) during which selling and drinking alcohol was prohibited (banned) in the USA.

Protestant   Of any Christian group that does not accept the authority of the Roman Catholic Church, but looks to the Bible as the source of religious truth.

race riots   Street fighting among members of different races who all live in the same community.

Regatta   A series of yacht and other boat races.

Republican   A member of the Republican Party, one of the two main political parties in the USA. Republicans generally have more conservative views than Democrats.

Second World War   A major war that lasted from 1939 to 1945 and involved a large number of countries. The Americans joined the war in 1941, fighting alongside the British, French, Russians and others to defeat Germany and its allies.

Senator   An elected member of the Senate, part of the US Congress (parliament). Each state elects two Senators.

shantytowns   Groups of poorly built shacks or shelters.

Star of David   A six-pointed star, the symbol of the Jewish religion.

sushi   A Japanese dish of raw fish on top of cooked rice, shaped into small parcels.

Tammany Society   The 19th-century New York Democratic Party that was based in Tammany Hall.

tenements   Large housing blocks divided into flats.

tuberculosis   A serious, infectious disease that causes fever and often inflammation of the lungs.

United Nations   An international organization formed in 1945, after the Second World War. It aims to promote world peace and so prevent further wars.

Wall Street Crash   A financial crisis that took place in the USA in 1929 and led to job losses and bankruptcies.

Washington, George   (1732-1799) A politician and general who was commander in chief of America's armies during the American Revolution (1775-83). He was then the first president of the USA (1789-1797).

INDEX